IN MY HEART ROOM
Book Two

More Love Prayers for Children

Mary Terese Donze, A.S.C.

LIGUORI
PUBLICATIONS

One Liguori Drive
Liguori, Missouri 63057-9999
(314) 464-2500

TO MARY
who taught the small Christ
to pray

Imprimi Potest:
James Shea, C.SS.R.
Provincial, St. Louis Province
The Redemptorists

Imprimatur:
Most Rev. Edward J. O'Donnell, D.D., V.G.
Auxiliary Bishop
Archdiocese of St. Louis

ISBN 0-89243-329-9
Library of Congress Catalog Card Number: 90-70810

CONTENTS

About this book

This second of two "Heart Room" books follows the plan of the first (*In My Heart Room*, 1982). The introductory pages are similar to those of *In My Heart Room*, making it possible to use this second book without referring to the preceding one.

The prayers need not be presented in any particular order; but if the children are new to the method, I suggest that "My Balloon Prayer" be taken before the others, since this prayer includes explanatory notes from the first book and introduces the children to the meaning of "in my heart room."

From time to time during the prayer sessions, the children are told to *think* something. While the word *imagine* might seem more appropriate to the process, I have used the word *think* deliberately. It keeps the prayer effort from falling into the same category as the fairy tales and just-for-fun mental exercises you might be using with the children at some other period of the day. I have likewise taken what I considered necessary grammatical liberties with the word *like*.

In some prayers there is random mention of children's names. You may want to substitute names from your own group. If so, make sure that over a period of time each child's name is mentioned at least once.

Give particular attention to the first prayer session with the children, since much of the success with this method of contemplative praying will depend on how carefully and devoutly the children are led through their initial prayer experience.

The Author

INTRODUCTION
Can Little Children Pray in Their Hearts?

Can you teach little children to meditate prayerfully, to "think in their hearts"?

The answer is yes. Not only can they be taught to pray in this manner we deprive them of a profound spiritual experience if we fail to teach them this type of prayer.

Parents and teachers can lead very young children into relatively deep, yet easy, forms of prayer by following a simple procedure. This procedure includes a *concentration exercise, meditation,* and *contemplation* — big words, but simple in application.

In *concentration* the children are trained to focus their entire attention on one object and to dismiss any other thoughts.

In *meditation* the children continue to concentrate on the object but are directed toward thoughts related to the subject.

During the *contemplation* phase, the process of thought-gathering ceases. Now the children are quietly led to *identify* with the object or with some situation involving it. At this point the children can relate in a personal way to God or Jesus in their hearts. The children make no effort to speculate on anything at this time. They simply rest in attentive awareness of God's closeness to them.

The following pages contain sixteen such depth-prayers for children six to eight or ten years old. Each prayer is given in its finished form; it may be read to the children directly from the page. With time, however, you should feel free to develop other themes with the children, following the same technique.

The prayers are addressed to a classroom group of very young children but may be used with the individual child. With suitable adaptations, this same method of praying may be used with older children and with adults.

NOTE TO
THE PRAYER LEADER

Before giving directions to the children, make sure they are comfortably seated. If the prayer session is being held in the home or in an area of the school that is carpeted, the children may sit (not lie) on the floor.

Help the children relax by taking them through a few breathing exercises. Direct them to breathe deeply and slowly (and silently) through the nose, in and out several times.

If this is the children's first experience with this type of prayer, be sure they have been prepared beforehand by some short discussion of what they are going to do. Be brief. It is sufficient that the children realize that they are praying and that it is a time of quiet.

After the children have been prepared, begin the instructions. If you are standing, do not move from place to place as you read the prayer directions. Use a calm, quiet tone that is audible without being loud. Try to read as if you were speaking. Appeal to their hearts but avoid the dramatic. State the direction in a simple, sincere way, keeping in mind your desire to lead the children to God through this prayer. Pause between sentences or parts of sentences where the thought suggests a pause but avoid prolonged silences. Move through the prayer with a certain deliberateness.

It is up to you, the prayer leader, to determine how often you will use this type of prayer. Every day seems too frequent. Once a week may be enough to have the children grasp the technique. Also, if you see a response that would justify repeating a certain prayer because the children like it or ask for it, follow that lead.

Study your group as you proceed. If the children are unable at first to sustain the effort required, shorten the procedure. But do not change the approach. Little by little they will begin to find the method easy and delightful and will look forward to the prayer sessions with joy.

After the children have been using the method for some time, allow them to offer suggestions for prayer. Guide these suggestions; work out the three-phase prayer pattern so that the venture does not fall flat. On the other hand, do not minimize the action of the Holy Spirit in the hearts of the children.

Finally, begin well. Approach each prayer session asking God to bless you and the children you are trying to lead to him.

1
MY BALLOON PRAYER

Preparation for Parent or Teacher

At the beginning of the prayer period, have a helium-filled balloon displayed in a prominent place but securely fastened so it does not bounce against the ceiling or move about the room. Have another balloon that is not inflated.

Renew your own "good intention" before starting this prayer.

Concentration Phase

NOTE: The concentration phase is meant to help the children become practiced in focusing their minds on an object — a balloon, a top, or with older groups, a Scripture text.

Tell the child(ren): Have everything off your desk for a while. Now sit tall so your back feels good. You will feel good all over, too, if you make your breath go in and out, easy and slow, like this: in...out...in...out. *(It is important that the children under-*

stand this type of breathing and do not interpret your words to mean loud, sniffy breaths.)

I have a balloon in my hand. (Show the children the balloon that has not been blown up.) It is a lovely balloon, but you can't tell it is lovely because it is flat. If we want to make it go up into the air like the other balloon, we have to fill it with a special kind of gas.

Meditation Phase

NOTE: In the meditation phase, you try to enrich the child's mind with positive thoughts related to the object.

Close your eyes now and think that you have filled a bright yellow balloon with this special kind of gas. The balloon is big and beautiful and has your name printed on it. You go outside holding the balloon by its string. You walk along, and the balloon floats over your head. Then, because you want to, you let go of the string, and your balloon flies into the air. You watch it go. It looks even more lovely sailing up against the blue sky. And because it is your balloon, it was you who made this beautiful thing happen. But you could not have done it without putting the special gas into the balloon. (Pause at intervals during each prayer period to allow the child to relish the thoughts that you are trying to evoke.)

Contemplation Phase

NOTE: In the contemplation phase, you try to help the child become aware of and communicate with God in a simple, sometimes wordless, manner. "Sitting at the feet of Jesus and listening to him" — this is the attitude you hope to foster in the child.

Keep your eyes closed now and think that you go into your heart room, that little place inside you where you sometimes go

12

when you want to be all alone to think. Each of us has a place like that inside our hearts. It is a quiet place to be because nobody ever gets inside this little room except you and God...Jesus. Jesus is always there. It is his special place where he waits for you. He takes care of you from there. But he is very quiet, and you don't always notice he is so close to you. See Jesus in your heart room now. He is happy that you are coming to be with him. Hear him say your name. Go close and stand beside him. Feel him put his arm around you. Listen to him talking to you. He will not speak words you can hear with your ears, but if you stay very quiet, you will hear him in your heart.

"My child," he is saying, "sometimes the things people do, their good actions, are like a little flat balloon. Not really a balloon, of course, but like it. *(The occasional "not really" expression is an effort to help the child grow in an understanding of symbolism in prayer.)* What makes their good actions like a flat balloon is that something special is missing in them, something that keeps them from going to God, to me, just like the special gas missing in the flat balloon keeps it from going up into the sky.

"But Alice, Jamie" — hear Jesus say *your* name — "I will tell you how you can make everything you do, all your actions, be something good and beautiful and be lifted up to God, to me. All you need do is think in your heart before you do something: 'Jesus, I do this for you.' Grownups call it 'making a good intention.' That means having a good reason for what you do. I, Jesus, am a very good reason for what you do.

"So when you eat your cereal for breakfast or when you read from your book at school or even when you go outside to play, think to yourself, 'I am going to do this all for Jesus.' It will be your good intention. It will put something special and beautiful in all you do and lift it up to me. If you do this often enough, you will soon get into a habit of offering everything you do to me.

13

You might ask my mother Mary to help you get into this habit. She always remembered to make a good intention."

Listen now while Jesus keeps on talking to you. "My child, someplace in your books there is a story about a man named King Midas. Everything he touched turned to gold. Of course, this is only a make-believe story. Nobody can ever touch things into gold. Anyway, it didn't work out for the king, and he got into a lot of trouble. But each time you say, *'All for Jesus,'* it is like turning things into gold because you get rich graces in your heart, and I put aside a special surprise that will be waiting for you when you get to heaven."

Stay quiet awhile with Jesus. Then tell him you love him and want to do everything for him. Ask him to help you remember to say often during the day, "Jesus, this is all for you." Ask him, too, to help you to get into a habit of making this good intention.

Closing Moment

It is time to come from your heart room. Open your eyes slowly and begin to breathe quietly in...and out...in...out. *(Allow time for each child to come out of the contemplation phase at his or her own rate.)* As you open your eyes, think right now that you are going to do everything for Jesus today and that you will ask Jesus' mother to help you remember to say "All for Jesus" until it becomes a habit with you.

(On the chalkboard where the children will be able to see it all day, write or print: Jesus, I will do this for you. *Refrain from making comments on what you have written. The children's own prayer experience will enrich the thought it suggests.)*

2
MY ANGEL PRAYER

(The doctrine of the Guardian Angels is not explicitly defined as one of faith, but devotion to the angels is deeply rooted in Catholic tradition. And the Church does celebrate a feast day in their honor on October 2.)

Preparation for Parent or Teacher

Post a picture of the Guardian Angel. This particular prayer session supposes the use of the traditional picture of an angel guarding two small children crossing a bridge. If you are not familiar with this picture or are unable to find it, adapt the Concentration Phase to fit your picture. But avoid using pictures or posters of chubby, baby-faced cherubs that are rightly cute but do not capture the spiritual. The children need to sense the strength and protective care of the angel.

"Angel of God...guard...and guide me."

Concentration Phase

Tell the children: Sit very quietly. You will want to hold your head tall so your back is straight up and down. This will keep you from getting tired and will help you to think better. Let your hands and feet rest, too.

Begin to breathe in a quiet, peaceful way — long…easy …breaths that are too soft to hear but that make you feel very good.

Look at the picture. The person who painted it gave the angel wings. Angels really do not have wings. They don't need them. They can get places in a hurry without them. But the artist painted the angel that way to remind us that angels go fast to do whatever God tells them to do. The angel is watching over the children. The angel does not want them to get hurt. The children are not afraid. They know the angel loves them and is taking care of them.

Meditation Phase

You may close your eyes now and keep breathing very softly. Think that you see Mr. President leaving the White House where he lives and getting into his car. He is going on a trip. There are some men going with him. Each time the president goes somewhere, these men go with him. They are his security guards. They watch over him and protect him. They get paid much money for doing this.

God has given us angels as our security guards. They watch over us. They especially watch over our souls so the devil may not hurt us by making us do wrong things. Of course, the angels could help us from hurting our bodies, too, like not smashing our finger in the car door. But *mostly* that is what our parents do for us: they see that our *bodies* don't get hurt.

The angels keep watch that our *souls* don't get hurt. The angels do all this because they love us.

Contemplation Phase

Now you are ready to go into your heart room. Keep your eyes closed and think that you open the door to this quiet place deep inside you where Jesus always waits for you. See him sitting there and smiling when you walk up close. He knows you have been thinking about angels. Hear him say to you.

"Mary…John…" or whoever you are, "I made all the beautiful angels. They live in heaven. But they don't just stay there and be happy. They want to share their happiness. They want you to live in heaven someday and be happy there with them. And because the angels love you like that, I have told them that they may come and watch over you and fight away the devil when he gets near you and starts giving you bad ideas.

"The angels are very strong. When you see a picture of angels, you might not think they are strong. But angels are stronger than your mommy or daddy. They are even stronger than the women you see playing tennis or running in races or the men you see boxing or wrestling on TV. So you can be sure they will fight off the devil if you ask them to. Only you must listen to how the angels tell you to get rid of the devil. The angels will not talk out loud, but you will know in your heart how they are trying to tell you to be good."

See Jesus looking lovingly at you while he is talking. He is hoping you will understand how special you are to him, since he gives you a heavenly security guard. Think that you put your arms around Jesus and say to him, "Thank you, Jesus, for making angels and for letting them help us." Because none of us is strong enough to fight off the devil all alone.

Feel Jesus' arms around you, too, and stay quiet awhile longer, just being happy to have Jesus holding you close.

Closing Moment

Now you are ready to leave your heart room. Think of how you are breathing slowly...in...and out...without hurry. And because you know now how the angels help you, think that you will say "Thank you" to the angels whenever you remember them. Think, too, that sometime today you will look around and see if you can be like an angel and help somebody.

(Suggestion: Keep a large picture of the Guardian Angel in the classroom throughout the year.)

3
MY BED PRAYER

Preparation for Parent or Teacher

If you are a parent using this prayer at home with your child, you will have a bed nearby or in an adjoining room.

If you are a teacher in the classroom, you may want to collect enough colored pictures of beds from advertisements so each child can have one. Pass these out to the children at the opening of the prayer session.

As a last resort you may have a large bed drawn on the chalkboard. Be sure it looks inviting.

Ask for yourself the grace to grow in a proper reverence for all things.

Concentration Phase

Tell the children: When we pray, our hearts help us talk to God. But our backs and heads and hands and feet help, too. They help by being very quiet. Sit tall now and tell your hands and feet to stop moving and to take a rest.

Breathe in and out slowly...and softly....It will help your body keep quiet and feel peaceful.

Now look at the picture of the bed. It is a big bed and it looks soft and comfortable. Most people put a special spread over the bed during the daytime to make the bed look nicer. And beneath the spread is a blanket or a quilt to snuggle under and some cool sheets that smell fresh and clean.

Meditation Phase

Close your eyes now and think that you see a big soft bed. It is covered with a lovely spread. You look at the bed and think how very quiet it is. Beds are like that. That is what makes them different from chairs that can be pushed around or tables with noisy dishes or furniture with drawers that move in and out.

Maybe, too, beds are different because people do so much living in them. People sleep in them every night. Sometimes when people are tired, they go to bed even during the day. Sick people want to lie down on a bed.

Sometimes a bed becomes almost a holy place. A baby may be born in a bed, or people may want to lie in a bed when they are ready to die and go to God. Sometimes people who love each other but are very busy all day wait until they get to bed to say, "I love you." And some people even pray in bed. One little girl — we now call her Saint Therese — had a bed with curtains around it. She used to sit on her bed and pull the curtains closed so she could be all alone and talk to God.

Contemplation Phase

We are going into our heart room now to talk with Jesus. Keep your eyes closed. Think that you walk ever so softly to where Jesus is waiting for you.

Step up close to him. Feel him put his arm about you. Be glad to be with him. Talk to him about your own bed. Maybe sometimes you crawl under your bed to be alone or just for the fun of being all closed in by the covers hanging down. If you do that, tell Jesus about it. Or tell him if you like to jump up and down on your bed — except that when you get bigger, you know that isn't good for the bed. If you pray in your bed or sometimes even cry there, tell Jesus that, too, and why you cry. Because Jesus is God, he knows this already. But like your daddy, who always wants to hear *you* tell him something even if he heard it from someone else, Jesus wants you to tell him all these things.

Stay close to Jesus when you are finished talking to him. Be happy in the way he loves you. And before you leave your heart room, thank him for the way beds are so quiet and holylike.

Closing Moment

It is time to come out of your heart room. Open your eyes slowly and take a long, deep breath, quiet and easy...in...and out. Think that the next time you go to bed and pull the covers up around you, you will remember how you and Jesus talked about beds. And if you are big enough to make your bed when you get up in the morning, think that you will make it look very smooth and nice. It will be your way of thanking Jesus for giving us such special things as beds.

(In making comments at the end of a prayer session, keep the same quiet stance that prevailed during the prayer.)

4
MY APPLE BLOSSOM PRAYER

Preparation for Parents or Teacher

Before beginning the prayer period, be sure the physical surroundings are comfortable for the children.

Have ready a small blossoming twig from some fruit tree, preferably an apple tree, or a large picture of a fruit tree in bloom.

If you use the real thing, at the end of the prayer period place the twig on your desk or before some religious statue in the room. Never casually dispose of anything used in connection with prayer. There is no need to be sentimental; but if you are guided by a spirit of reverence for all things, you will know the difference.

Ask the grace to surrender your own soul to the changes necessary for your growth in holiness.

Concentration Phase

Tell the children: Sit tall now…your feet on the floor…your hands resting quietly. We are going to take some slow, easy breaths as we always do…in…out…in…out…in…out. And for a little while we are going to think about these apple blossoms.

This is a twig from an apple tree. It is full of blossoms. See how small and dainty each flower is. *(If necessary, move about the room to allow each child an opportunity to see the flowers up close.)* If these little flowers hadn't come out, no one could ever have guessed they were hidden inside this stick of wood. What is even more wonderful, the flowers will turn into apples if the little tree keeps growing.

Meditation Phase

Now close your eyes. Think how pretty a whole tree full of these blossoms would be. Each year that is what happens to an apple tree. It gets full of flowers like this and looks like a big, lovely bouquet. Then one day the flowers begin to fall off the tree.

Think that you see them now. The wind is blowing them off the tree. It scatters them on the ground. Soon none are left on the tree. If the tree could talk, maybe it would say that it is sorry to lose all its pretty flowers. It doesn't know that it has to lose the flowers if it wants to keep on growing into a good apple tree.

A few weeks after the flowers are gone, a small green bump, like a hard pea, is growing at every place where there had been a flower.

Then summertime comes, and these small green bumps get bigger and bigger. By the time summer is over and you are back in school, the bumps have grown into shiny red apples. *Now —* if the tree could talk — it would say how happy it is for the apples.

But the apples wouldn't have come if the tree had not given up its flowers and let itself grow into something bigger and better.

Contemplation Phase

Keep your eyes closed. Think that you go into your heart room. Jesus is waiting for you there as he always is. See his face brighten when he sees you. He is happy that you have come. Walk up to him. He has something to tell you. Stand close and feel his arm around you while he talks.

Think that he says to you, "Jennifer," — or Eric or Dawn — "you are like the apple tree with its flowers. Sometimes you have something you like and you want to keep it. Then the thing you like goes away as the flowers did, and you are sad. But mostly when it's that way, if you let the nice things go, something still nicer comes afterward.

"It is like the time when you had a loose tooth and wished it hadn't gotten loose because you couldn't bite hard things without its hurting. But then you let the loose tooth go, and soon a bigger and better tooth grew in its place. Or it is like being happy in the first grade and being afraid to leave and go to the second or third or fourth grade where you won't know how to read the hard books. And then after a while, you are in the fourth grade and can read the hard books. You like it and would not want to go back to the first grade.

"But it is not always easy when we have to give up something we like. Some people find it hard to give up even a pair of old shoes that they're used to. So come to me whenever you find it hard to give up something. We will talk about the apple tree and about how we have to change if we want to grow better."

Stay awhile longer with Jesus. Keep thinking a little more of what he told you about having to change. Now you are ready to leave your heart room. Feel Jesus lay his hands on you to bless you. Be happy in his blessing.

Closing Moment

You may start to come out of your heart room. Breathe softly and quietly in…and out…. Before you open your eyes, think that you want to remember in your heart how the apple tree had to give up its flowers if it wanted to have apples. Ask Jesus' mother, the Holy Virgin Mary, to help you remember all this. She used to remember things in her heart, too. And if you know a boy or girl who is unhappy to give up something, maybe you could help by telling that boy or girl the story of the apple tree.

(This could be made practical for the children if a new child has transferred to your school and misses his or her friends from the other school.)

5
I TELL MY SINS TO JESUS

Preparation for Parent or Teacher

The following prayer presupposes that the children have been instructed on the manner of "going to confession." The prayer may be used before the children's first confession or before any later reception of the sacrament.

In preparing the children for the confession of their sins, avoid anything that would fill their minds with fear or uneasiness. Be sure they have not only seen the confessional or the place where they will meet the priest but also have moved around in it, touched it, knelt or sat where they will later be. And while it is important that they feel at home with the priest, it is equally important that they realize that God has called this person in a special way to take away our sins in Jesus' name. Speak reverently to them of this great task that Jesus has given to his priests.

If you have a picture of the Prodigal Son, post it where the children can see it. Public libraries sometimes lend out beautiful art prints.

When you take the children to confession, use your own judgment as to whether you yourself should approach the sacrament. Example has a powerful influence on children. By going to confession along with them, you may help them feel more secure. Whatever you choose to do, your personal practice in regard to the sacrament is vital to your leading the children to God through this great means of grace.

Concentration Phase

Tell the children: It is not always easy to be good, and sometimes we do things that are bad. If we do bad things because we really want to be bad, that is wrong. That is a sin. If I drop my dinner plate and it breaks, it is a pity because maybe it was such a nice plate. But it is no sin. Or if I run around the corner of the house and bump into my little brother and knock him down, I did not do anything bad, even if he hurts his arm and cries.

But if I get mad because I don't want to eat something on my plate and I throw the plate on the floor, or if I push my little brother down or hurt him because I am mad at him and I want to hurt him, that is different. That is a bad thing to do.

Most of us feel unhappy when we have done something bad. A little voice inside us keeps telling us we shouldn't have done what we did. If we really love Jesus, we begin to feel sorry about the way we acted because we know he doesn't want us to act that way. We wish we could undo the bad thing and start over.

Jesus knew we would feel like this, so he thought up a good way for us to start over. He gave his priests the power to take our sins away. Of course, Jesus forgives us the minute we are sorry, even before we go to the priest. But he still wants us to go to the priest so we can hear with our own ears when the priest tells us our sins are forgiven. We don't have to *guess* that *maybe* Jesus has forgiven our sins. No, it is for sure because Jesus said it would be that way.

Today (tomorrow) you will be telling your sins to the priest. But before you do this, I want to tell you a story. Close your eyes now and sit straight and think about breathing a few quiet, way-down, easy breaths, slowly, in and out. In…out…in…out. *(Do this three or four times until the children are relaxed.)*

Meditation Phase

(I have adapted the story of the Prodigal Son for the very small child. If you are using the prayer with older children, you may want to use the gospel story as it is.)

Once there was a big boy whose daddy was very good to him. But the boy did not want to stay with his daddy. He didn't like to do what his daddy told him. So he asked his daddy for some money. After he got the money, he ran away from home. He stayed away for a long time. He spent his money to buy whatever he liked, even if it wasn't good for him, and he did some bad things, too. But after a while his money was all gone. He felt unhappy. He remembered how good his daddy had been to him and how he shouldn't have run away and smarted off the way he did. He began to be sorry. He wished he hadn't been so bad. He wanted to go back home.

His daddy still loved him. You could tell that because every day his daddy went out into the front yard and looked down the street to see if he could see his boy coming home. But he never saw him.

Then one day his daddy looked out the window and saw a big boy walking up the driveway. The boy was very dirty, his clothes were ragged, and he needed a haircut. The daddy knew at once that it was his boy. He ran out the door and down the driveway to meet the boy.

When the daddy got close, the boy started saying how sorry he was and would his daddy take him back, please. But his daddy was so glad to see him that he didn't even let him finish talking. He threw his arms around him and took him in the house and got him cleaned up and then had a big party for him. It was wonderful. Everybody was happy.

Contemplation Phase

Keep your eyes closed. Think now that you go into your heart room where Jesus is waiting for you. See him smile as you enter. He is happy to see you. Think that you walk up close to him. Feel him put his arms around you. You like it when he does that. You like to feel his arms around you.

As Jesus holds you close, tell him all the naughty things you did, all the sins, the same things that you are going to tell the priest in confession. Speak out. You never have to pretend with Jesus. Tell him you are sorry about all these things because you love him and you know he died on the cross to help people not do bad things anymore. Ask him to help you start being better. *(Pause where you feel the children need time to think.)*

Now listen to Jesus. Hear him tell you that when we sin, we are like the boy who ran away from his good father. Hear Jesus tell you he is that good Father and that he loves you very much. Listen carefully, too, while he tells you that after you tell your sins to the priest and are sorry about them, they will all be forgiven. No matter what sins you did, after you confess them and are sorry, Jesus wants you to forget them FOREVER because they aren't there anymore; they are gone — just like a bubble that bursts. That bubble is gone for good. So will your sins be gone, and you can start loving Jesus all over again.

Stay with Jesus a little longer, not talking, just being happy with him, knowing that his arms are about you, that he loves you no matter if sometimes you aren't so good as you would like to be.

Now thank Jesus and ask him to help you to be truly sorry for anything bad you did and to remember what to say to the priest when you go to confession.

Closing Moment

Begin to breathe quietly, bringing in the air in long, easy breaths in...out...in...out....Think how when you go to confession, you will tell the priest just what you told Jesus because the priest takes Jesus' place and wants to help you just like Jesus wants to help you. Think, too, that you will ask our Blessed Mother to be near you when you say your sins to the priest. Having her near will be like having your mother near when you have something a little hard to do.

And when you meet the priest today or any day, thank Jesus in your heart for calling the priest in such a wonderful way to take our sins away.

6
My Eraser Prayer

Preparation for Parent or Teacher

The children will need an eraser before they begin this prayer. They may use their own erasers, or you may want to give each child a small pencil-top eraser. The color and newness may make it a more effective tool for prayer.

As you hand each child an eraser, take time to make a loving eye contact that says, "You are special." Children — indeed, all of us — are hungry for that personal interest of another that is truly Christ's presence to us.

Be grateful for the privilege of sharing in the Christian formation of the Church of the future.

Concentration Phase

Tell the children: It is good to feel rested when you want to think in your heart. Most often you will feel rested if you sit up tall and let your back straighten out. And while your back is straightening, you can breathe in a few easy, quiet breaths …in…out…in…out.

Pick up your eraser and hold it in your hand. Or if it is hard to hold because it is so little, slip it onto the end of your pencil and hold the pencil. See how small the eraser is; yet it is very useful. It helps many people.

Meditation Phase

Close your eyes now. Think that you see a woman writing a very important letter. She is writing to get a job. She is in a hurry and is not careful. She misspells a word. She reads over the letter and sees the misspelled word. She is sorry she allowed herself to make the mistake. She erases the wrong word at once and spells it right. She would not get the job if she could not spell correctly. The eraser helped her.

Or think that a man is printing some music. He is careless and puts down a wrong note. If someone played the music, it would not sound right. The man is sorry about the wrong note. He knows he shouldn't have put it in the music. He erases it and puts in the correct note. The eraser helped the man make the music sound lovely. *(If these two examples seem enough, skip the following paragraph.)*

Or think that someone writes directions on how to get to a friend's house. He is not careful and puts down the wrong street number. Then he sees that he wrote something that was not right. He is sorry. He erases the wrong number and puts in the correct number. The eraser helped him to tell someone how to reach the friend's house.

Each time, the eraser helped someone to correct something wrong and turn it into something right.

Contemplation Phase

Keep your eyes closed. Think now that you are moving into your heart room, that quiet place deep inside you where Jesus truly lives.

Think that you hear him calling you to come in and close the door so that you and he can be alone for a while. Walk up to Jesus. See him reach out his hand to draw you nearer to him. Let him hold you close the way you like someone you love to hold you.

Hear Jesus talking to you. "Julie, Jonathan, Megan" — whoever you are — "I want to be like a big eraser for you — not really an eraser, but like one."

Hear him keep on talking to you. "I want to help you erase all the wrong things you do and change them into good things. If a mean thought comes into your heart not to like somebody you *should* like...or not to share something with your little brother or sister...or to fuss about what Mother or Daddy tells you to do ...I want you to come to me in your heart room and tell me about it. And just as the eraser changed the wrong thing into a right thing, I will help you change the mean thought into a good thought.

"Each night before you go to sleep, come into your heart room and tell me about all the wrong things that happened during the day that you are sorry went that way. I will help you change how they went so that the next morning your heart will be ready for a good new day."

Think awhile about what Jesus has said to you. Ask him to help you always remember to come to him to have the wrong things made right again.

Closing Moment

It is time to come out of your heart room. Breathe a few quiet breaths in...and out...in...and out. You can open your eyes, too.

Look at your eraser. Think that when you use it today and the next days, you will try to remember how Jesus said he would make things right for you, just like an eraser lets you make wrong things right on paper. Think, too, that you will ask our Blessed Mother to help you remember all these things.

7
I AM GOD'S LEAF

Preparation for Parent or Teacher

Gather enough tree leaves for each child to have one. You can use leaves fresh from the tree. Or you might prefer to gather them beforehand, preserve them between two pieces of transparent contact paper, and cut them apart for the children when you are ready to use them. The preserved leaves are beautiful and have the advantage of not drying or getting limp. On the other hand, such preserved leaves deprive the child of the natural feel and smell of the fresh leaf.

You might compromise, using the fresh leaf — even if it is a bit withered — for the prayer session and giving the child the preserved leaf to take home as a reminder of today's talk with Jesus.

"Lord, open my lips, and my mouth shall proclaim your praise."

Concentration Phase

Tell the children: Sit tall and easy with your back straight. Begin to breathe good full breaths — but softly. Feel the air come in through your nose. Breathe it down toward your stomach. Then let it come out quietly. Do it again...in...out...in...out.

Now look at the leaf you have. It has a very special shape. No two leaves in the whole world are exactly the same. Not even two leaves from the same tree are alike. If you look carefully, you will see heavy lines in the leaf and smaller lines reaching out from them. These are the veins in the leaf.

The leaf you have is green, but sometimes the green leaves turn red and yellow and orange and brown, even purple, during the autumn. The colors make the leaves very beautiful. Leaves are also good for making shady places under trees where people can sit on hot days.

But it is not the shape nor the lines nor the color nor even the cool shade they give us that makes the leaves so special.

Turn the leaf over. On its bottom side are hundreds of little openings too small for you to see. But through these openings, or "mouths," the leaf is letting out into the air an important, good gas. We call this gas oxygen. We need this good gas each time we breathe. If we did not have it, we could not stay alive. It is truly life-giving. That is what makes leaves so special.

Meditation Phase

Close your eyes now and think that you are in a big woods. There are trees all around you. It is cool and shady in the woods because the trees are full of leaves. All the leaves are breathing out this special oxygen gas. They do it so softly that no matter how hard you try, you cannot hear them. But you can tell they are doing it because the woods smell fresh and clean and make you want to keep on breathing more and more of the life-giving air. Think that you keep standing awhile in this quiet woods, breathing in the good oxygen.

Contemplation Phase

Keep your eyes closed. You are ready to go into your heart room. Think that you are opening the door to this quiet place right now. It is even more quiet in your heart than in the big woods. Best of all, Jesus is there waiting for you. Go close to him. Feel him draw you to himself. He has something to say to you.

"Lisa...Kevin...you are my little leaf."

You know you are *not really* a little leaf, so you wait for Jesus to tell you what he means.

"The little leaf has many tiny mouths," he is saying to you. "Out of those mouths comes something very precious, something that is life-giving — the good oxygen gas.

"You have only one mouth, but it is enough. Out of your mouth can come something very precious, too. With your mouth you can say kind words to someone who is sad and feels dead-like inside. Your kind words will cheer the person who is sad and move the dead-like feeling away. Your words will be like the oxygen; they will be life-giving.

"Or with your mouth you can pray for people who do very bad things that kill off my life-giving love in their souls. You hear about these bad people every day on TV and on the radio and in the newspaper. Your prayers can make the bad people want to come back to me and be good again. You will truly have been life-giving for them."

Think now that Jesus tells you this story about someone who was life-giving for someone else.

Hear him say to you, "Once, when Saint Therese was no bigger then you, she heard her mother and daddy talking about how a man had done something very bad and was going to be hanged for it. At first the man didn't care that he had killed off God's life-giving love in his soul by being bad. Therese wished she could help him. She prayed very hard for the man because she didn't want him to die being so bad and not being sorry and then not getting to come to me in heaven. Because she prayed so hard, the man changed his mind. He started to feel sorry about what he had done. Therese's prayers had been life-giving for him."

Look at Jesus. Tell him now you understand about being a leaf. It means using your mouth to help others by praying for them or by saying kind and happy words to them. Ask Jesus to bless your mouth so it will always do these good things.

Closing Moment

It is time to come from your heart room. Begin to breathe softly like the leaves breathe...in...and out. Before you open your eyes, think once more how wonderful it is that God gave you a mouth that can say kind words and pray in ways that are life-giving for other people. *(Pass out the preserved leaves. When everyone has one, continue speaking.)*

You might want to pin up your special leaf somewhere at home where you can always see it. Tell yourself that each time you look at your leaf, or at any leaf, you will try to remember to be life-giving for someone else by being kind and prayerful. Ask our Blessed Mother to help you.

(Never elaborate on the remarks in the Closing Moment. You have done your part. Respect the child's relationship with God and hesitate to interfere with the action of the Holy Spirit.)

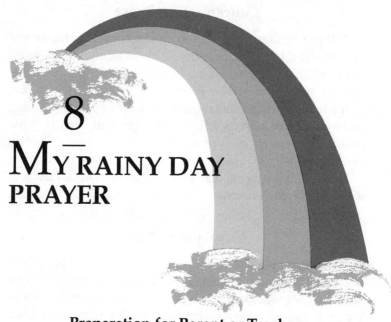

8
MY RAINY DAY PRAYER

Preparation for Parent or Teacher

Use this prayer on a rainy day. If the weather is warm, have the windows open so the children can see and hear and smell the rain as you speak to them.

If possible, somewhere prominent in the room have a picture of a real rainbow. Most small children are familiar with the stylized colored bow from books and advertisements, but quite a few have never seen even a picture of a real rainbow in the sky.

Since children are more restless on rainy days, make a special effort to move about and speak in a calm and relaxed manner. Keep your eyes gentle and accepting of each child before you. In everything related to prayer, take a quiet and reverent approach.

Concentration Phase

Tell the children: Sit up tall so the stack of little bones in your back has a chance to line up straight without being crowded. You can rest your hands...easylike...and your feet are best on the floor. Now we are going to take a few quiet breathes, soft ones...and slow...in...and out...in... and out....They help to make us feel good all over. *(Let the children spend a minute or so — no longer — gently breathing.)*

While you are breathing, look out at the rain....Listen to it....You can smell it, too.

Meditation Phase

Close your eyes now, and we will think about the rain. There is something wonderful about how rain comes down the way it does. It is not squeezed tight together like the water that comes out of the faucet or the drinking fountain. The rain comes down in little drops.

When you look through the rain, the little drops do not have a pretty color. They look gray. That is why some people don't like the rain. They want something that is bright and cheery and makes them happy. The gray rain makes them sad.

Maybe some things make you sad, too. Maybe they make you feel just like there's a big rainy day in your heart.

But if we had no rainy days, we would be missing something very beautiful because some rainy days end in a wonderful surprise. Sometimes the sun comes out before the rain has time to stop falling, and all at once the raindrops are no longer gray. They are red and orange and yellow and green and blue and purple. They were that color all along, of course, but the sun had to shine on them in a special way before their beautiful colors showed through. Then they spread across the sky like a big bridge. We call it a rainbow.

Contemplation Phase

Keep your eyes closed. We are going to talk to Jesus about rainy days. Think that you open the door to your heart room. There is Jesus, sitting right there waiting for you. Walk over to him. See him reach out his arms and let you sit on his lap. Lean your head against his shoulder. Don't say anything for a while.

Then hear Jesus say, "Jessica, Dick, or Jason" — or whatever your name is — "what is this about rainy days?"

Speak out to Jesus. Tell him how sometimes, after someone has hurt you or you have done something you shouldn't have done, you feel like a rainy day, all sad inside.

Feel Jesus lay his hand on your head and hold you close. Hear him say to you, "Tommie," — or "Mary" or "Jack" — "when you are sad and your heart feels rainy, come to me. We will talk about what makes you sad, and I will help you get the rainy feeling to go away. I will be like a big bright sun for you. I will shine on the rain and make it become a rainbow in your heart. Be sure to come, no matter what makes you sad. I always want to make you happy because I love you very much."

For a while think that you rest your head against Jesus' shoulder and feel how nice it is to be loved. Thank Jesus for always wanting to bring out the best things in you, like the sun brought out the colors in the raindrops.

Once more listen to Jesus talking to you: "Today, or any day, if you see somebody looking sad, be a big bright sun for him or her, just as I will always be a big bright sun for you. Smile at that person so he or she will be happy and a rainbow will shine in his or her heart."

Closing Moment

It is time to leave your heart room. Thank Jesus again and tell him you will always come back to him when it gets gray and rainy in your heart.

Open your eyes now. And remember that you are going to try to make a rainbow shine in somebody's heart today — maybe Grandma's heart or the heart of the boy or girl who sits next to you in school or your little sister's heart.

. *(If you have small rainbow stickers, give one to each of the children with some such suggestion as: "You might want to put this up someplace to remind you of what Jesus said to you today.")*

9
MY GARDEN PRAYER

Preparation for Parent or Teacher

In the front of the room where all can see it, have a picture of a lovely garden. Or have small pictures of flower beds or gardens to pass out to the children. Sunday magazines, with their colorful floral advertisements, and plant catalogs are good sources of such pictures.

Concentration Phase

Because the buildup in the prayer session is toward the Contemplation Phase, there is a tendency after a while to put less emphasis on the other phases, particularly on the Concentration Phase with its relaxation techniques.

However, to go routinely through this part of the prayer preparation or to underestimate the need for passive bodily participation in prayer may cause the prayer itself to be less effective.

Animate yourself, therefore, with a spirit of calm reverence toward the body as you take the children through this section of the prayer exercise.

Tell the children: Sit tall with your head up. Pull your chin in and up a little until it feels free and cool and lines up your neck straight with the bone in your back. You may want to tell your feet to rest quietly on the floor and your hands to lie still. We don't have to talk out loud to our hands and feet to get them to do this. We just think it in our mind, and our hands and feet understand. Begin to breathe softly and slowly in...and out...and in...and out.

Now look at the picture of the garden. See the colors of the flowers. They are pink or white or yellow or red or purple. Some of the flowers are tall and some are short.

Whoever planted this garden must have worked hard to keep it beautiful because gardens can't grow nice by themselves. People have to plant them and water them and pull out the weeds.

Meditation Phase

Close your eyes now. Think that it is the beginning of summertime and you are walking through a beautiful garden. You see all the lovely flowers beginning to grow. The roses are already blooming. You touch their soft petals. Everywhere around you is the sweet smell of the flowers. The owner of the garden has planted the flowers and watered them. You see a few weeds in the garden. But they are very small. It will not be a hard job for the owner of the garden to pull them out and keep the garden beautiful.

Think now that you have been gone away all summer. Then, at the end of summer you come back and visit the garden once more. It is no longer beautiful. The owner did not bother about the little weeds. They grew to be big and tall and ugly. It will be very hard to pull them out. Many of the flowers will be pulled up with the weeds because they are growing so close together. What a pity! You remember how lovely the garden looked in the beginning of summer, and you are sad. If only the owner had pulled out the weeds when they were little!

Contemplation Phase

We are ready now to go into our heart room. Keep your eyes closed and think that you open the door and walk slowly over to where Jesus sits waiting for you. He smiles to welcome you. Go close to him. Maybe today you feel like you would like to sit at his feet and rest your head against his knees while he talks to you.

Listen to him call you by name and say to you, "My child, your soul is like a garden. Not really a garden, you know, but like one. You want to keep your soul garden beautiful, and I want to help you keep it that way. Each time you do something good, it is as if a flower starts to grow in your garden. The more often you are good, the more beautiful the flowers get. I am the one who plants these flowers for you, and I water them with my grace." *(Do not be concerned if the children have not yet been told of grace. They will get the overall idea.)*

"But the devil and sometimes bad boys and girls want to put weeds in your garden. They tell you to do something bad. If you do the bad thing and then are sorry right away and don't do it again, it will be like a little weed that you can pull out of your heart garden in a hurry. But sometimes bad people keep bothering you and bothering you until they get you to do bad things over and over again. Then the weeds grow big and strong and ruin the lovely garden of your soul.

"A man named Judas who was once a friend of mine had a

lovely garden in his soul. Then he began to steal money — at first just a little. But he kept on doing it until he was stealing more and more. The weeds grew and grew in his heart garden until there were no flowers left at all.

"If Judas had been sorry and had come to me, I would have helped him pull out the weeds — it would have been hard, but if he trusted me, we could have done it. But he got to thinking he had been too bad for me to like him anymore. And the devil made him nervous and told him it was no use. Judas believed the devil and never came to me. He went away and killed himself. It was very sad; I could have helped him because I loved him.

"Another friend of mine named Peter let a lot of weeds grow in his soul, too. But then he got very sorry and came back to me to help him get good again. Soon the garden of his soul was once more full of lovely flowers.

"Keep away from bad people. Say 'No' to them. And don't listen to the devil when he tells you to do something wrong. But if someday it should happen that you get started doing something bad and you keep on doing it until you are being bad almost all the time and your heart garden is full of big weeds, be like Peter: come to me. Don't let the devil make you nervous and afraid. Never, NEVER think that you are too bad to come to me. Even if the weeds are as big as trees, I will help you cut them down and make your heart garden beautiful again."

Think now that you get up from where you are sitting and kneel at Jesus' feet. Look up into his face and smile to let him know you like the way he is so good. Ask him to bless you.

Closing Moment

Begin to breathe softly in…and out…and in…and out…and come out of your heart room. Before you open your eyes, think how tonight — and maybe every night — before you go to sleep you will try to remember if you let any weed grow in your heart garden by being bad during the day. If you did, tell Jesus you are sorry about it. And — just like that — the weed will be gone, and the flowers in your heart garden won't be hurt. Ask our Blessed Mother, too, to help you be careful about the little weeds, the little sins.

10
A VALENTINE FOR JESUS

(If Valentine Day comes on a Saturday or Sunday, you might use this prayer the preceding Friday.)

Preparation for Parent or Teacher

Place a statue or picture of the Sacred Heart where all the children are able to see it. Do not use a picture of a heart only. The child's devotion should be to the "whole" Jesus.

Ask that your own heart experience a deepening of love for the sacred humanity of Christ.

Concentration Phase

Tell the children: Remember how the long bone in your back is made of little bones, one on top of the other? Sit tall so these small bones rest nicely in their places. It makes your whole back feel good. Begin to breathe quietly. And while you breathe in...and out...in...and out...think to tell your hands and feet to stay very still.

Because it is (will be) Valentine Day today (Saturday/Sunday), people everywhere are giving each other some kind of hearts: paper hearts or red candy hearts or chocolate hearts or cookie hearts. When people give a heart to someone, it is their way of saying, "I love you."

Today we are going to think about Jesus, who loves us and gives us his heart.

Look at the picture (statue) of Jesus. See his heart. Our hearts are inside us. Jesus' heart is inside him, too. But the person who painted this picture (made this statue) put Jesus' heart on the outside where we can see it. It looks like flames of fire are coming from Jesus' heart and a band of sticky thorns is wrapped around it. On top of Jesus' heart is a cross.

Meditation Phase

Close your eyes now and I will tell you a story. Then you will know why the person who made the picture (statue) showed us Jesus's heart on the outside of him.

A long time ago there was a very holy woman. She was a nun (Sister). Her name was Margaret Mary. She loved Jesus very much. He loved her, too. They were very good friends. One day Jesus came to visit Margaret Mary. He stood right in front of her. When she looked at him, she could see straight into his heart. It looked like it was full of a lovely fire burning with a warm, beautiful light. There was a cross on top of his heart and a ring of thorns around it.

Jesus pointed to his heart and told Margaret Mary he loved all of us so much that his heart felt like it was on fire with love. You will know what Jesus meant if you remember how you feel when you love somebody. Your heart seems to get all excited. It beats

49

very fast, and there is a nice warm feeling inside you as if the love in your heart is really like a little fire.

Of course there wasn't any *real* fire in Jesus' heart. You can't have a fire inside you like that. So Jesus' heart didn't hurt from a fire. But it did hurt because some people don't care that he loves them. It was like your loving somebody and wanting that person to love you and maybe whoever it was didn't love you. Your heart would hurt, too.

Then Jesus pointed to the thorns and the cross. It was to remind us of how much he had suffered for love of us. A lot of people who lived at the time when Margaret Mary lived had forgotten about Jesus' dying for them. They had forgotten that he loved them very much. Jesus asked Margaret Mary to remind everybody again of how much he loved them. So Margaret Mary told as many people as she could what Jesus said to her and how Jesus' heart looked.

Ever since that time when people paint a picture of the Sacred Heart of Jesus, they put Jesus' heart on the outside to remind us of what Jesus said about how much he loves us.

Contemplation Phase

(The following exchange between Jesus and the child can be very intimate. Pause frequently to allow for this possibility.)

Go into your heart room now. Jesus is waiting for you. Think that you walk up very close to him. Feel him put his arm around you. Think that you lean your head on his shoulder. You keep remembering what Jesus told Margaret Mary about how much he loved all of us. You remember, too, that it is Valentine Day, a Love Day, when people give hearts to each other to say, "I love you."

Hear Jesus ask you for your heart. That means he is asking you to love him. You are very special to Jesus. There is nothing in the whole world that he wants more than your heart. Offer it to him. Tell him that you want your heart to belong to him always.

See Jesus look lovingly at you and hear him say, "My child, I give you my heart, too." Be very happy because that is Jesus' way of saying, "I love you."

Tell him that you are sorry when his heart aches because some people don't love him. Tell him that you will try to love him even more to make up for the way those people don't care about him. And if somebody *you* love doesn't love *you*, tell Jesus that, too. He will try to make it up to you because he doesn't want *your* heart to ache either.

Stay with Jesus a little while longer. You need not talk. People who love each other don't always need to be talking. Sometimes they just sit and hold each other's hands and don't say anything.

Closing Moment

Come out of your heart room now. Begin to breathe softly, in and out. Look at the picture (statue) of Jesus once more. Think that each time you see a picture or a statue of the holy heart of Jesus you will say to him, "Jesus, I give you my heart." And remember he said he gives you his heart, too.

Think, too, that if you see somebody looking sad or standing alone with nobody to play with, you will be nice to that person so his or her heart won't ache.

(If you have small holy cards of the Sacred Heart and know they would be meaningful to your group, you may want to give each child one of the pictures. Briefly suggest they keep them on their desks during the day to remind them that they and Jesus have given each other their hearts, their love, today.)

11
MY LIFE-SOUL PRAYER

(See note at end of this prayer.)

Preparation for Parent or Teacher

If possible, have a large picture of Christ's Resurrection placed where all the children can easily see it. Alternatively, you might give each child a small holy card of the Resurrection. Or you might want to do both. In any case, do not attempt this prayer without some tangible Resurrection image for the child to fasten onto.

Before beginning the prayer, repeat your own humble act of faith: "I believe in the resurrection of the body and life everlasting."

Concentration Phase

Tell the children: Clear your desk except for the holy card about Jesus. Sit tall. Let your feet be quiet on the floor and rest your hands in your lap. You will want to breathe in and out through your nose. Feel the air come in. Breathe it down deep in soft, easy breaths in…out…in…out. *(This prayer is longer than usual. Make sure the children are comfortable.)*

Look at the picture of Jesus. Once upon a time some bad men who did not understand Jesus killed him. The happy, lovely thing that had kept Jesus alive went out of him for a while. He was dead. His friends who loved him took his body and put it into a grave. But Jesus came alive again, and today he is happy and feels better than he did before they killed him. Best of all, he will never die again.

And that is what all of us want — someday to come alive as Jesus did, never to die again.

Meditation Phase

Close your eyes now. For a while we are not going to think about Jesus being dead and then alive. Think instead that you are watching a little plant grow. It is very small at first. Then it gets bigger and bigger. The flower on it opens and smells very sweet. The plant does all this because God has put a life-thing inside it. No one has ever seen this life-thing, but it is there. Some plants live a long time; others die after a few days or weeks. When a flower dies, it is because the life-thing, the thing that made it be a flower, went out of it.

It is the same about a little dog. It can jump and bark and wag its tail and maybe even do tricks. It can do all these things because God has put a life-thing in it. But when the life-thing goes away, the little dog dies.

If it were your little dog, you might look at its dead body and say, "That is not my *real* dog." And that is true. Your real dog was the dog that was alive and jumped around and was fun to be with. What you are looking at now is *part* of your dog, the part you could see. But its life-thing has gone away. So we dig a big enough hole in the ground where we can lay the part that is left of our dog and cover it over. But we don't bury the nice life-thing that really made our dog be a dog. That thing is someplace else for a while.

God put a life-thing inside people, too. It is a very special kind of life-thing. We call it a soul. Nobody has ever seen a soul inside someone else, but it is the thing that makes us alive and helps us walk and play and laugh and eat and have fun with each other. It helps us to think and to read and to do arithmetic. Most of all, God puts this life-soul in us so we can learn to know and love him and someday be happy with him in heaven.

But when people get old or very sick or in an accident, sometimes their bodies can't walk or eat or laugh or breathe anymore. Their life-soul can't get them to do anything. Their bodies are too tired to move. So the life-soul lets the body rest for a while and goes back to God where it came from.

It's like if our grandpa would die. We would look at him and say, "That is not my *real* grandpa. My real grandpa smoked a pipe and laughed a lot and gave me things." And that is true. This is only part of Grandpa, his human body. But the life-soul that made Grandpa really be Grandpa is gone. It went back to God.

Because we loved Grandpa, we put his human body into a casket, and the priest blesses him and prays for him. Then we lay his body to rest in a grave in the cemetery. But someday God is going to put back the life-soul into Grandpa's body and into the bodies of all the dead people, and then their bodies will be like new, and the life-soul will never again leave them. They will live forever.

Nobody knows on what day God will come and lead the life-thing away from the plant or from the little dog or the life-soul from Grandpa. But God is the one who puts the life-soul into us, so we can be sure he knows when is the very best day to take it out for a while. We need to trust him.

Contemplation Phase

Go quietly into your heart room. See Jesus waiting for you. Go up close to him and feel him put his arm around you. He is happy that you came to talk to him about being dead because he knows more about it than anyone else.

Listen while he tells you how having to die got started.

"John, or Marcia," or whoever you are, he is saying, "a long time ago I made Adam and Eve, your first parents. I loved them, and they loved me. And they were very happy. But one day the devil told them to do something wrong, to commit a sin. The devil knew that if they did this bad thing, they would have to die and their life-soul would not go to heaven. The devil is like that, mean and ugly, and always wanting to spoil things.

"Adam and Eve should have known better. But they went ahead and did what the devil told them, and right away a death-thing got into them and after that into everybody else. The devil was happy. He was glad Adam and Eve had to die, and he wanted them and everybody else to stay dead forever and never get to heaven. But I felt sorry for Adam and Eve and for everybody else. So I died on the cross to make up for everybody's sins so that they could come alive again and be happy forever in heaven.

"When I was dead on the cross, the devil even wanted me to stay dead forever. But he could never keep me dead. I am Jesus. I am God. I came alive again. I came right out of the cemetery and walked around and met my friends. And I am still living today and will never die."

Feel Jesus put his hand on your head now, softly and loving-like. He has one more thing to tell you. Listen again. Hear him say, "Tommie, or Billy, or Jane, when our dog dies or somebody we love dies, we don't get to go along with them, and our hearts feel very sad. We miss them. Most often we cry. Sometimes we cry very hard. It is all right to cry. It helps us feel better. I cried once when my friend died. But I am talking to you now and telling you all this so you won't *keep on* crying because now you know that death is not for good. Someday everyone will come alive again."

Closing Moments

Come out of your heart room. Begin to breathe slowly. Open your eyes. Look at your picture. You can take it home with you. Each time you see it think of what Jesus told you: how someday all of us who love him and who love our grandpas and a lot of other people will have our life-souls back in our bodies and will live together in heaven with him forever.

NOTE: This prayer deals with the concept of death. Use your good judgment as to when or if you should use it with the very small children. At the same time, it is useless to shield them from the fact of death. They see it on TV and hear about it every day.

It is better that they get the correct notion about this great mystery from a loving parent or teacher rather than from the media or being left alone to try to figure out for themselves what death is all about. Children are often more perceptive than we think, and the Holy Spirit is not inactive in their souls.

Be prepared for some child to ask whether his or her pet goes to heaven when it dies. Probably the most satisfying answer for the small child — indeed valid for any age — is that when we get to heaven, if we still think we need a dog or anything else at all to make us happy, God will be sure to see that we get it because God wants everybody happy in heaven. (No need at this time to explain how our concept of happiness will differ by the time we reach heaven.)

If you use the prayer with older children (who may ask about animal "souls"), you might briefly explain — to the extent of their ability to comprehend — that when animals and plants die, the vital principle that kept them alive reverts to the potentiality of matter. Don't invite questions but be prepared with answers.

12
MY SNOW PRAYER

Preparation for Parent or Teacher

While it seems ideal to take this prayer on a "snow day," it will also be a challenge, since children are fascinated by the sight of falling snow — especially if it comes down in large, loose flakes — and it may be difficult for them to keep their eyes closed or to give their attention to anything but the falling snow. You may need to wait until the snow stops or take the prayer later in the day when the children have had ample time to watch the snow. Let your decision depend on the emotional involvement of the children.

If you are using this prayer in a locality where it seldom or never snows, you might post a large snow scene someplace where the children can easily see it. (Calendars are often good sources of such pictures.) You may also have to make slight adaptations in the prayer.

Concentration Phase

Tell the children: You will want to get your feet and hands rested before we start. Your back will feel rested, too, if it is straight and tall. And now begin to breathe those slow, easy breaths that help us feel quiet inside. In...out...in...out...in...out.

Look at the snow. *(If the children cannot see the snow from where they are seated, you might begin by saying:* Think about how the snow is coming down outside.) It is very clean and more white than anything else. It is soft, too, like fluffy feathers. And no matter how hard it snows, it is never noisy like rain.

Snow is pretty when it is all together. But each flake is beautiful by itself. We can't bring the snow inside to examine it because it would melt. But when you are outside, if you let the flakes fall on your gloves or scarf, you will see that each snowflake has a different shape and looks like a tiny, fancy star.

Meditation Phase

Close your eyes now. Keep thinking about snow. Some people don't like it because their cars get stuck in it and they can't get to work and then they don't get paid for that day. Some people don't like it because they have to bundle up and go out in the cold and shovel the snow off their sidewalks.

But the snow does many good things for us. It sticks on trees and bushes and makes us think of Christmas. In some places the snow lies on top of high mountains and makes them pretty against the blue sky. Snow covers the farmer's grainfield and helps his wheat when it melts. If there is enough snow on a hill, it gives grownups a chance to use the skis that they had stored away all summer. Snow makes old people who can't go outside happy to watch it from their windows. And for children snow is good for snowballs and snowmen and for riding on a sled.

Nobody knows for sure why God thought of making snow, but almost everyone is happy that he made it.

Contemplation Phase

Keep your eyes closed. You are going into your heart room now. See Jesus waiting there for you. Hear him call you by name and tell you to come up close to him. Feel him put his arm around you. He is glad to see you.

Listen now while Jesus talks to you. "Laurie, or Gloria, or Kirk," — or whatever your name is — "I made the snow. I knew when I made it that it would be fun to play in. It pleases me to see you happy making snowmen and snowballs and riding on your sled. Maybe you even know how to lie in the soft snow and stretch out your arms to make 'angel wings.'

"Most people who are not too grown up like snow. They like the way it is so white and quiet and gentle. They like the fun it makes, too. And because they like it, they tell me, 'Thank you, God, for making the snow.' A lady named Mary Dixon Thayer remembered all the good times she had in the snow when she was a little girl, so she made a special prayer to thank me for snow. You can ask your teacher to tell you about the prayer. *

"Another lady said that the snow reminded her of my mother Mary because my mother is so quiet and gentle and her soul is so clean and pure. So each time it snowed this lady thanked me for my good mother."

Keep standing close to Jesus. Put your hand in his and thank him for letting you be with him and for giving us the snow. Tell him that you will ask the teacher about the snow prayer that one lady made up so you can say it, too. And if you like what that other lady did, you might want to tell Jesus that whenever it snows, you, too, will think of his dear, pure mother and of how gentle she is and will thank him for her.

Stay a little longer with Jesus. You need not say anything. Just think how you love him and how he loves you.

Closing Moment

It is time to come from your heart room. Breathe soft and easy and begin to open your eyes. And while you are breathing quietly and opening your eyes, I am going to say that "thank-you-for-snow" prayer that lady made up.

(Do not read the prayer to the children. Have it memorized beforehand so that it comes spontaneously to your lips — and from your heart.)

If the snow continues, you might interrupt what the children are doing several times during this first snow day — especially if they are getting tired or restless — and break into a spontaneous recitation of the snow prayer — no formal "let-us-pray" thing, but a sudden lifting of the heart. Encourage the children to pray along with you but do not hold up the prayer for them. This seems a better way for them to learn the words than for you to actually teach the prayer by rote. And the children will like the sudden surprise of your stopping what they are doing and talking to God. Don't overdo.

(Suggestion: Some time before the winter season is over, you may want to teach the children to cut snowflakes from folded paper. It is a good exercise in illustrating how no two snowflakes are alike.)

* MY WINTER PRAYER

The world is covered up with snow
Today, dear God! I want to go

And play in it before the sun
Comes out and melts it. O! What fun

It is to be a child today!
"Thank You!" Is all that I can say!

"Thank you, dear God, for trees that stand
And shine like trees in Fairyland!
Thank you for the blue of the sky!
Thank you for a cloud going by!

Dear God, this is my Winter Prayer —
"Thank you for snow-flakes, everywhere!"

— Mary Dixon Thayer

13
MY CURTAIN PRAYER

Preparation for Parent or Teacher

Tape a large picture to the front chalkboard or someplace where the children will have no difficulty seeing it. Do not use a picture with religious significance. Colored scenery or some neutral subject will do. Be sure it is beautiful. You will not be using it as part of the prayer session, but beauty has its own religious effect.

Have a piece of cloth taped or hung so that it falls loosely down and covers the picture like a curtain.

Before beginning the prayer with the children, ask the Holy Spirit to arouse within your own soul an abiding hunger and thirst for the vision of God.

Concentration Phase

Tell the children: When we want a plant to grow up tall, we sometimes tie it loosely to a strong stick. The stick helps the plant keep straight.

The long setup of bones that God put into our backs are something like that stick. It helps us stand and sit tall. Feel your backbone helping you sit tall now. And let your hands and feet get quiet and at rest.

There is a big picture on the chalkboard. *(Indicate with your hand.)* It is a very pretty picture. You can't see it because it is hidden behind a curtain. But even though you can't see the picture, you believe it is there because you hear me telling you about it.

Now I am going to take away the curtain. *(Remove the cloth.)*

With the curtain gone, you no longer have to *believe* the picture is there. You *know* it for sure. You can see it and enjoy it. *(Do not spend time on the picture once the children have seen it. Go immediately into the Meditation Phase.)*

Meditation Phase

Close your eyes now. Think of how the curtain hid the picture. And while you remember the curtain, I am going to tell you a story about a man named Fulton Oursler.

When Fulton was a little boy, he did not have many friends. He was lonely. One day an old lady told him that God was in the church. Fulton thought God would be nice to have for a friend, so he ran down the street and went into the church. He looked all around. When he couldn't see God, he thought God might be hiding someplace. Fulton crawled behind the big church organ, where it was dusty and full of spider webs, looking for God. But he never found him. Fulton felt very sad.

The old lady had forgotten to tell the little boy that God, Jesus, is truly in the church in holy Communion but that we can't really *see* him until we get to heaven. And she forgot to tell him that Jesus was also in his heart room.

But in church and in our heart room, it is like God is behind a curtain. We don't see him, but we believe he is there because Jesus has told us it is true. Someday when the curtain is taken away, we won't have to *believe* this any longer. We shall see God, Jesus, and know him just as he is.

You will understand this better if ever you have gone to a theater where they had a big stage with a curtain. You will remember how you waited for the show to begin, how you waited for the curtain to be pulled aside. You knew wonderful things were going to happen when that curtain was moved away. It is something like that with Jesus in the church and in our hearts: we know he is there even if we can't see him. But someday the curtain will be gone, and there before us will be heaven and Jesus, God.

Contemplation Phase

Keep your eyes closed now and go quietly into your heart room. Think that you walk over to Jesus and that he puts his arm around you as he always does. Listen to him tell you that someday all the things that are like curtains will be taken away, and then you will see him just as easily as you can see your mother or daddy when you are at home. You will be able to see the color of Jesus' hair and his eyes. You will hear how kind his voice is and feel his hand gently on your head. *(Be sure to pause at intervals during the prayer.)*

Hear Jesus tell you that MOST of all you will see something about him better than you could ever guess — you will see his *Godness*. Nobody can tell you how being God happens in Jesus, but it is what makes Jesus different from everybody else and makes all of us love him and trust him and need him so much. In heaven Jesus' Godness shines out all over him and makes him so special that the angels never stop saying over and over how great and holy and wonderful he is.

When you get to heaven and see Jesus' Godness, you, too, will want to keep telling him, "Jesus, you are great! You are extra special! You are the best God there ever could be. I love you very much." And then Jesus will do something else you never could have guessed: he will share his Godness with you and make something of God shine out in you.

Before you leave your heart room, hear Jesus say to you, "When the day comes, Mary" — or Janet or Jeremy — "there will not be a curtain between you and me anymore. You will not have to speak to me in your heart room or in holy Communion. You will speak to me face to face, and I will love you, and you will love me, and I will be your God-Jesus forever."

Closing Moment

It is time to come from your heart room now. Begin to breathe the easy, long breaths that help you keep a quiet and happy peace inside. Start to open your eyes. Think that when you say your prayers tonight before you go to bed — and maybe some other times, too — you will ask our Blessed Mother, who is full of Jesus' Godness, to help you to love Jesus more and more and to keep doing what he wants you to do so that someday in heaven you, too, can be filled with Jesus' wonderful Godness.

14
MY GOD-IN-THREE-PERSONS PRAYER

Preparation for Parent or Teacher

As with the Life-Soul Prayer, this prayer challenges the minds of the children (and minds other than those of children). Be sure to have read and prayed over the prayer before you try to present it. Avoid rushing any of the sentences.

The prayer is structured to avoid emphasis on the words "Holy Trinity" as being too abstract for the children and therefore not evoking a love-of-God response. For the same reason, it seems best not to show the children any symbol of the Holy Trinity (a shamrock, for example) lest, in view of the abstract concept, they fasten onto the symbol.

Concentration Phase

Tell the children: When we begin to pray, we most often say, "In the name of the Father, and of the Son, and of the Holy Spirit."

67

(The teacher might make the Sign of the Cross while saying these words.) That is the same as saying, "In the name of God, and of God, and of God," because God is three Persons, even though he is one God. *(Don't expect the children to follow your every thought; but if you proceed slowly and prayerfully, they should get an overall idea of God's unique nature.)*

Nobody understands how this can be because it is a mystery of God. We call this mystery of Persons in God the mystery of the Most Holy Trinity — three Persons, one God. Even though we can't understand this mystery about God, we can think about how it might be.

Before we start to think about this, you will want to get quiet and ready to think. Sit so that those special small bones in your back stack up straight and make you feel comfortable. And when you have your hands and feet rested, begin to breathe deep and easy breaths in…and out…and in…and out.

Meditation Phase

Close your eyes now. Before we think of how God can be three Persons, we are going to think of how your own daddy is like three persons — not really the way God is three Persons, of course, but something like it.

When your daddy goes into the basement and gets some wood and a saw and a hammer and some nails and begins to build shelves for Mother to use in the kitchen, your daddy is like a builder-person. Then, if he gets into his car and goes to work at the store or the shop or the office and does things for other people all day long, he is like a helper-person. And in the evening when he comes home from work and hugs you and plays with you and lets you know how glad he is that you are his little boy or girl, he is like a love-person. You could look at him and say, "My daddy is like three different persons, but he is still my one daddy."

Contemplation Phase

Keep your eyes closed. Go into your heart room now. Walk to where Jesus is waiting for you. Now sit very quietly at Jesus' feet and listen carefully while he tells you about God-in-three-Persons but just one God.

Hear him say that when you pray "In the name of the Father," you are speaking of God, our heavenly Father, who built the whole world.

Then see Jesus pointing to himself and saying, "And when you say 'and of the Son,' you are speaking to me, of Jesus, who died on the cross to help everyone get to heaven."

(The content of the next sentence is difficult. Take care not to rush through it, even though the children won't understand it. The manner in which you say it will make its impression.)

"When you say 'and of the Holy Spirit,' you are speaking of God's life-giving love that keeps God being our Father and me being God's best-loved Son and the Holy Spirit loving the Father and me and uniting us all as one.

"This God-being-three-Persons will always be hard to understand. Philip, one of my apostles, wanted to know more about 'the Father, the Son, and the Holy Spirit.' So one day he asked me to show him the Father.

"I told him, 'Philip, you are looking at the Father right now because when you see me, you are seeing the Father, since the Father and I are one and the same God.'

"It was like with your daddy again. If you had said to your daddy when he was building the shelves, 'I want to see my love-daddy,' he would have smiled and said to you, 'You are looking right at your love-daddy because your builder-daddy and your love-daddy are the same daddy.' "

Hear Jesus keep on talking. "If you love me, you will understand all this better than if you sit down by yourself and try to think about how it can be. It is always that way. When we love someone, our hearts tell us more about that person than what our heads with all their thinking can tell us."

Before you leave your heart room, see Jesus raise his hand and bless you. Thank him in your heart that he has told you about God being one in three Persons. And be glad that there is no other God besides him.

Closing Moment

Begin to come out of your heart room. Breathe happy, easy breaths in...out...in...out...and slowly open your eyes. Think that each time you make the Sign of the Cross and say, "In the name of the Father, and of the Son, and of the Holy Spirit," you will thank God in your heart for how special God is who can *truly* be three Persons and still be just one God. Think, too, that you will always make the Sign of the Cross carefully to honor God for being so wonderful.

15
MY I-AM-SPECIAL-TO-GOD PRAYER

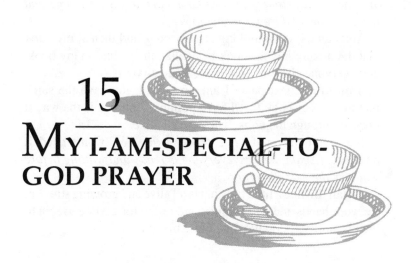

Preparation for Parent or Teacher

If you are the teacher using this prayer with the children, have ready your copy of the children's reader (primer).

If you are using the prayer with an individual child at home, use anything of which you have a double: similar teacups, a set of candlesticks, the drapes on the windows, and so forth. But confine yourself to speaking of one set only.

Recall with joy your own uniqueness and dignity in God's sight.

Concentration Phase

Tell the children: You will need your reader for a little while. *(Give them sufficient time so that when you start, everyone is ready.)*

Now open your reader to the first page where there is a picture and look at it. *(Hold your own book open at the first page and turned so the children are able to see it.)*

You can tell from looking at your book and then at my book that the picture in your book is just like the picture in my book, and everyone else's picture is the same as yours.

Turn to the next page. I am sure all of you have the same picture in your book that I have in mine. And that is the way it goes all through the book. They are all alike.

Now you may put your reader away. We won't need it anymore. *(Again, be sure everyone is ready and waiting before you give the next directions.)*

Sit tall. Be like a little tree that is all alive and growing straight. Let your hands and feet be quiet and rested for a while. Begin to breathe softly...slowly...in...out...in...out.

Meditation Phase

Close your eyes and think that you are going into a store where there are all kinds of toys. You might walk up to the clerk and say, "Please, where are the dolls? I want to buy two that are just alike." And he would say to you, "Go to the next aisle. You will find a whole shelf full of dolls." Or if you want to buy two of the same kind of baseball bats, the clerk would say, "Go over there to the sports aisle and you'll find a lot of bats."

You could even buy ten dolls or ten baseball bats that looked alike — if you had enough money. It is the same with the dolls and the bats as it is with the books; hundreds of them are alike.

But it is different with people. You could not find hundreds of *them* alike; they really aren't. Each one of them is a different person. And each of them isn't anybody but just himself or herself.

Contemplation Phase

Keep your eyes closed. It is time to go into your heart room. See Jesus waiting for you. See him smile. He is happy to see you. Go over to where he is sitting. Let him hold you close. Be very quiet with Jesus for a while.

Then listen to him say to you, "Jill" — or Steve or Shirley — "there is no one in the whole world like you. I never made two people alike. Somebody may have a name like yours, but it won't be you. I made everybody different so that there would be only one of each person and not ten or twenty or a hundred like all those dolls and baseball bats.

"Since you are the only one person like you, that makes you special. And because everyone else is just himself or herself and nobody else, that makes everyone else special, too, but each in a different way. None of the boys or girls in your class is like anyone else in the class. Some of them are tall, some have curly hair, some have dark skin, some have blue eyes. I made everybody different because I wanted to love each of you one by one just for yourself.

"And I want you to love me, too, because if you do not love me, I won't have anybody like you to love me, since there isn't anyone else around like you."

Before you leave your heart room, hear Jesus say one more thing to you. "Jerry" — or George or Marcie — "if sometimes you start thinking you aren't very important, and you wonder if everybody else feels that way about you, too, remember that *I* think you are important, and you will always be special to *me*."

Closing Moment

It is time to come out of your heart room. Begin to breathe in and out slowly and quietly. Before you open your eyes, think once more of how Jesus said you were special to him and how he would miss it if you didn't love him. Think, too, that you will always be nice to other boys and girls and everybody else and treat them as special so they won't ever have to feel like they are no better than a lot of dolls or baseball bats.

16
M̲Y̲ MAGIC WORD PRAYER

(Before using this prayer with the children, it would be helpful if they were able to recognize the printed form of "Jesus.")

Preparation for Parent or Teacher

If you feel it proper to include a bit of "mystery" in connection with the name of Jesus to help enhance its superiority over other words, you might want to post the optical illusion pattern of the name of Jesus where one sees and then does not see the holy name. (See illustration on page 79.)

However, the whole purpose of the prayer can be compromised if this "gadget" becomes the focus of the child's interest. To prevent this from happening, post the placard AFTER the prayer session is over and not necessarily immediately. Make no comments on the cleverness of the card. Simply tack it up and let happen what will. The placard is sure to become a topic of discussion among the children as soon as some child sees the holy name and another sees nothing but strange markings.

The placard is simple to make, but it is suggested that you resist the idea of having the children make their own. When we begin to manipulate "mystery," it ceases to exercise its power over us. However, you may want to supply each child with a print of his or her own. *

Before beginning the prayer with the children, renew your faith in the power of the holy name of Jesus.

Concentration Phase

Tell the children: Inside everyone's chest *(lay your hand on your chest)* are two lungs. When we breathe in, the air fills our lungs and then goes to all parts of our body to make them feel good.

If we sit hunched up, our lungs get squeezed together and cannot take in as much air. That is why when we think about it, we try to sit tall and straight. Now begin to breathe in the air...slowly...quietly...in...out...in...out.

Whenever you look inside a dictionary *(if you have one handy, hold it for the children to see),* you will find lists and lists of words. The dictionary tells you what the words mean. Some of the words are short and some are long. One of the long words is *abracadabra.* The dictionary says it is a word that some people once thought had magic power.

Meditation Phase

Close your eyes now. We are going to think awhile about *abracadabra,* that magic word. A long time ago when people first heard about this strange word, they thought they would try saying it to see if it worked any magic for them. They started saying *abracadabra* over and over and waiting for something nice to happen. But everything stayed the same; nothing extra nice ever happened. Soon they stopped saying the word. Now the only place you ever hear of anyone saying *abracadabra* and expecting wonderful things to happen is in make-believe stories. People read these stories for fun. They laugh because they know they are not true.

But there is a word that is *not* make-believe and that does wonderful things for us. That word is the holy name of Jesus. In the Bible — the big book that tells us all about God — Jesus is called the WORD, the Word of God. A word is something we use to express ourselves. To express ourselves means to think in our minds and then to say what we were thinking. To do that, we need words. Like with our name. We think in our mind who we are, and then we tell other people who we are.

Jesus is called the WORD because it was the best way God could express himself — know himself in his own mind and then tell us about himself.

Contemplation Phase

Keep your eyes closed and go ever so quietly into your heart room. Jesus knows you have been thinking about special words. Feel him put his arms around you. Listen, now, while he talks to you. Feel how good it is — the way he talks in your heart.

Hear him say now that he is your *true* magic Word. Each time you say his holy name, Jesus, devoutly — devoutly means you think of Jesus and love him when you say it — something wonderful will happen for you.

Jesus knows you cannot guess what really wonderful things will happen, so listen while he tells you.

"Bobby" — or Erin or Terry — "each time you say my holy name, each time you say 'Jesus,' I will put more and more love into your heart. I will do more than that. I will take away your sins and give you grace to help you to be good. If you say my holy name when the devil is trying to make you do something you shouldn't be doing, he will leave you alone and go away because my name is so powerful that he is afraid even to hear it. Keep saying 'Jesus,' and someday I, Jesus, the most Holy Word of God, will open the gates of heaven for you.

"A man named Saint Bernard loved to say my name. He said it over and over. He told people that my holy name was sweet to him, like honey on his lips."

Stay awhile longer with Jesus. Think that you go close to him and whisper his holy name lovingly into his ear two or three times before you leave him. Maybe someday Jesus will make his most holy name seem like honey or sweet candy on your lips, too.

Closing Moment

It is time to come from your heart room. Before you open your eyes, think again of how great and powerful is Jesus' holy name. Think that you will often repeat this sweet name in your heart. Ask our Blessed Mother to help you remember to do this. Ask her, too, that Jesus' name will be the very last word you say before you stop talking when you are ready to die.

---

* Bookmarks illustrating this feature are available from Franciscan Missionary Union, 1615 Vine Street, Cincinnati, OH 45210 (513) 241-4386. The paper bookmarks are free — unless you choose to make a small donation — but be sure to include a stamped, self-addressed business-size envelope. Write to Franciscan Missionary Union for information on other available items.

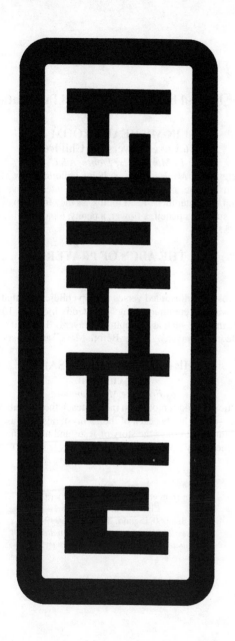

Other helpful books from Liguori Publications...

IN MY HEART ROOM
16 Love Prayers for Children
by Mary Terese Donze, A.S.C.

The original *In My Heart Room* helps children draw closer to
Christ using the same unique style of contemplative prayer.
Children will enter their "heart rooms" as they focus on everyday
objects such as a pencil, a flower, a penny, a piece of bread, and
others. **$1.95**

THE ABC's OF PRAYER
...for children
by Francine M. O'Connor

This book uses illustrated verses to help children see that prayer
is our way of communicating with God. Includes 13 actual
prayers-in-verse such as "Happiness Prayer," "I'm Sorry, Lord,"
"My Bedtime Prayer," "Prayer Before Mass," and others. **$2.50**

THE ABC's OF THE ROSARY
...for children
by Francine M. O'Connor

This little book does more than merely teach the formula and the
prayers — it highlights each of the 15 mysteries in a fascinating
presentation that brings the story of Jesus and his mother to life.
Makes the rosary a prayer experience the whole family can share.
$2.50

Order from your local bookstore or write to:
Liguori Publications
Box 060, Liguori, MO 63057-9999
*(Please add $1.00 for postage and handling for
orders under $5.00; $1.50 for orders over $5.00.)*